SONGS, BLOOD DEEP

GWEN NELL WESTERMAN

Poet Laureate of Minnesota

HOLY COW! PRESS
Duluth, Minnesota

2023

Cover watercolor painting, "The Musician" by Roy Boney, Jr., *www.royboneyart.com*
Book and cover design by Anton Khodakovsky.

Printed and bound in the United States.

ISBN 978-1737405146

First printing, Fall, 2023.
10 9 8 7 6 5 4 3 2 1

Library of Congress Cataloging-in-Publication Data
Westerman, Gwen, author.
Songs, blood deep / by Gwen Nell Westerman.
First edition. | Duluth, Minnesota : Holy Cow! Press, 2023.
LCCN 2022005155 | ISBN 9781737405146 (trade paperback)
LCGFT: Poetry.
LCC PS3623.E84767 S66 2023 | DDC 811/.6 23/eng/20220—dc07
LC record available at https://lccn.loc.gov/2022005155

Holy Cow! Press projects are funded in part by grant awards from the Ben
and Jeanne Overman Charitable Trust, the Elmer L. and Eleanor J. Andersen
Foundation, The Lenfestey Family Foundation, The Woessner Freeman Family
Foundation, and by gifts from generous individual donors. We are grateful to
Springboard for the Arts for their support as our fiscal sponsor.

Holy Cow! Press books are distributed to the trade by Consortium Book Sales &
Distribution, c/o Ingram Publisher Services, Inc., 210 American Drive, Jackson,
TN 38301. For inquiries, please write to: Holy Cow! Press, Post Office Box 3170,
Mount Royal Station, Duluth, MN 55803.

Visit *www.holycowpress.org*

For our granddaughters'

granddaughters'

granddaughters.

CONTENTS

PTAŊYETU

SONGS, BLOOD DEEP

My grandma told me
that her grandma told her,
that her grandma told her,
"When we came over
the top of the world,
there were already people here."

Beyond seven generations
times seven generations,
we have carried this history
and passed it on to the next
generation, in our blood,
and in our songs.

I heard my grandma's grandma's
grandma's story again, two years
after she left this world.
The sustained symmetry of songs,
blood deep in our mitochondrial DNA,
showed the world what we had always known.

FIRST SONG

Sitting on a quilt made
from her husband's work pants,
spread out on the ground behind
the house he bought for her,
on a late autumn afternoon,
my grandma taught me to sing.

     U ne la nv i u we tsi

     I ga go yv he i

     Hna quo tso sv wi yu lo se

     I ga gu yv ho nv

Then she told me
it is a sin to be greedy,

    to hoard

    when others are needy.

Always share something,

    always—

    a cup of coffee

    some wild mint tea

    just a glass of water

    a bowl of soup

    a few boiled eggs

    a piece of bread

    a clean towel

    some warm socks

    a spool of thread

    a length of calico

some dried corn

a bit of meat

a wooden spoon

a small pail

a basket

a gentle touch

a prayer

a song.

Nothing fancy,

just a token

that we care for each other

in good times

and in bad.

Share,

not give or take,

but share

whatever you have

no matter how small.

To accept a gift is

to know

how we are related,

to understand

our need to be connected,

to learn

how to receive love

even if we think

we don't deserve it.

BLOOD MEMORY

Once, in school they taught us that
    Navajo mothers buried
    their babies' umbilical cords
    beneath the hogan threshold
    so they would always know
    where home is.
My mother kept my siblings' cords,
black shriveled little twigs, in a small box
along with their baby teeth and diaper pins.
Once, I asked her, where is mine?
    Oh, she said, I threw it away
    a long time ago.
Perhaps that explains the feeling
that I did not belong there;
    why I wondered how a different family might be;
    why I wandered through books or on my bike, alone;
    why I left home at 17 and never really went back;
    why I migrated north to Kansas City where
once, at an art show,
    I bought a watercolor of a bluff
    resplendent with fall colors,
    wondering how I knew that place
    that seemed like home.
I wandered farther north where the bluffs
    along the Minnesota River,
    resplendent with fall colors,

were exactly the same

as the watercolor I bought years before,

and somehow, I knew this place.

Once, I stood across from the bluff

along the Minnesota River,

offering food and prayers

when the soles of my shoes

seemed to dissolve.

My feet and the ground were joined,

gentle hands reached up,

grasped my ankles and anchored me there.

I knew this place where the land

claimed me,

no longer wondering,

no longer wandering,

I was home.

COVALENT BONDS

we are

dream carriers

child bearers

those burdens borne

with hope

and intensity

under the gravity

of responsibility

history and

love

not guilt

love

and hope

for those who

will dream

and share

these burdens born

we do not give up

willingly

but attract and repel

balance and share

stronger

in that bond of

love

ANCESTRAL JOURNEY

Along a busy highway
in a new mown field,
a sandhill crane family,
parents with two young,
feed in the yellow stubble.

On guard, one adult stands tall,
watching intently
over the land at sunset
as the two small ones
move along the rolling ground.

Unaware of the traffic,
they prepare to rest
for the long journey ahead,
mapped into their cells
along this ancient flyway.

LOST HORIZON

Fog on a crisp fall morning
softens the sharp edge
between the earth and the sky.
No separation
truly exists between us/them.

CROW KNOWS

Crow glistens iridescent
in late morning sun
amid fallen leaves
along a busy street
where dying grass and concrete
intersect.
Drivers rush
halt
rush
halt
a blur of steel
and rubber
their eyes staring straight ahead.
Scarlet maple leaf
in his beak,
Crow admires its radiant beauty
in the late morning sun
amid the dying grass and concrete,
the blur of steel and rubber,
and winks.

HARVEST PHANTOMS

Birds settle in the cornfield
as evening draws near.
They rustle the drying leaves,
hop from stalk to stalk
then stillness covers the land.

In the dark, sounds of combines
blow over the fields.
Dried leaves of cornstalks skitter
down the road like ghosts
under the waning moonlight.

OCTOBER MORNING

My dog walks with me
early this morning to sounds
of gravel crunching
under our feet on the lane,
barred owls calling in the woods.

Across the ravine,
the sun rising through the trees
creates coral clouds
that fade to yellows and whites
as crickets sing to greet dawn.

Dust lays like a fog
over the newly cut fields
of corn and soybeans.
Cornhusks ride the breeze like birds
as three crows chat on a fence.

TRANSITIONS

Crisp as the cool air,
apples ripen on the trees.
In the still green grass,
deer feed on the fallen ones
with autumn slipping away.

After the harvest,
the fawn has lost its white spots
and stays near its mom,
eating corn left in the field
and growing strong for winter.

THE IMPERMANENCE OF LIGHT

A surprise among the grass
after a soft rain,
a purple flower appears,
its center a star
shining in the waning sun.

Perhaps Monet was inspired
by such simple sights,
red leaves floating in the grass,
subtle changing shades,
the impermanence of light.

PERSEVERE

Full harvest moon shines brightly
in the western sky,
still wrapped in the dark of night
just before the dawn,
anticipates the new day.

Cottonwood trees are now bare
after high, straight winds
ripped through the reds and yellows,
exposing branches
to the encroaching winter.

Hummingbirds are gone.
The songbirds left weeks ago.
A tundra swan stands
alone in an empty field
as the setting sun burns gold.

When our dream seems blown off course
by a single breath
from some unknown time or place,
its flight may be straight
to even more fertile ground.

DETERMINATION

A lone wounded goose
works against the changing winds
that bring down the cold,
searches for a place to rest
with his flock as the sun sets.

WANIYETU

ONE A DAY

is good for vitamins,
apples, horoscopes,
sunrises, famous quotes.
Just one,
only one.
Counting
minutes hours
people in lines
ahead of or behind us
insults,
perceived or real,
numbering
our grudges,
ordering our lives.
Looking out
for number one,
hearing second is
another word
for loser.
One way
One right
One and
only one,
just one.
What do we
lose
by counting
just one,
and only one?

SOURCE CODE

Brittle leaves

tap tap

at windows

their congregation

turns twirls

tumbles toward

the source

of life

tap tap

at windows

tap tap

a binary

twisting turning

writing plain

text while

leaves fall

like rain.

PANDEMIC WIND

November storm turns sharp
      and deadly frigid.
Before I can reach the house,
      leaves fighting to hold on
lose their last fragile connections
and are blasted beyond the yard.

What holds us here in the brunt
      of unseen forces?
Our connective threads ravaged,
      we struggle to hold on
to everything we thought we knew
      and are dying in the cold.

FACES

We looked at the faces
of the young girls in
their lacy white dresses and hats.
It must have been a special day
when a travelling photographer
made it up the road
from Bunch to their home.

Grandma pointed to the smallest girl
and said to me,
"This is my cousin Mary Mankiller.
These are her sisters.
I named your mother Mary
because she looked like her
when she was born."

Aunt Liza took the postcard photo,
looked at the faces
and then said to her,
"Your granddaughter there
looks like our mama Sallie.
But Mary named her
for you."

LAST PHOTO

after William Carlos Williams

so much depends

upon

a single

face

in a yellowed

photo

now glazed with

tears.

NOVEMBER 16

A grandma's birthday—

      100 years today, already gone twenty.

When I told you your sister Liza came

and stood at the foot of my bed,

      you said it was because

she was thinking

      of me when

      she died.

Your sister Katie too, then,

      I suppose,

when she appeared in the hallway

while I was watching TV.

      She smiled, her lips

      Cabana Red,

then disappeared.

When the phone rang

and they told me you were gone,

      I didn't know

what to say.

They said your last words were

I don't even feel like

      I'm alive.

There was no visit to me in the space

between here and beyond when you left.

Who were you thinking of then?

WINTER BURN

Lifeless cornhusks
are driven away
by a relentless wind,
remnants of a life
no longer useful.

Without warning,
ice crystals scatter
across the wind rows
and shatter
the last remnants
of warmth.

GIVING THANKS

By proclamation
of a president
the people will
give thanks.
What has happened to
a people who must
be ordered to
give thanks
on a given day
for overabundance
surrounded by
distractions
of food preparations
plastic decorations
smiling amid
red and yellow leaves
ignorant of
the sacrifices
ultimate
betrayals
by proclamation
of a president
of a people who first
gave thanks.

NOTHING BUT THE TRUTH

"Power concedes nothing without a demand."
— *Frederick Douglass*

Power concedes even though
the majority did not rule,
debunked stories repeated
as fact become
"alternative truth."

Nothing without or within
can progress beyond fear,
turning struggle into process,
unblurring lines between fact
and fiction.

Then a demand to be heard,
to be recognized,
to take active measures,
and to recover what
truth really means.

storyteller, *noun.*

defn: 1 narrator. **2** liar. **3** informant, as in oral history.
Also, stool pigeon, sneak, mole, spy.

If that is how
Mr. Webster
defined and described it
in these United States
of America,
it is no wonder
our storytellers
have no place
here.

Our defn: 1 culture keeper. **2** tradition bearer. **3** rememberer,
as in oral history. Also teacher, helper, moral compass, poet.

That is how
our sources
define and describe it
in these Indigenous
homelands,
where wonder
and story
make a place
for all of
us.

CONVERSION CONVERSATIONS

Hekta ahaŋna
dena eyapi.

They said,
"We come to share our love of God.
Teach us your language."

We gave you our hand, in friendship.
We gave you our God, in love.

They said,
"We come to take the land
you gave us in our treaties."

We gave you our names, in trust.
We gave you our word, in belief.

Then they said,
"Now we will tell your stories
in our own language."

We had nothing left to say.

SONG FOR THE GENERATIONS: DECEMBER 26

we rise

together

singing

our prayer

as one

hear us

we are

here

standing

at the

center

see us

we do

this

today so

our people

will live

tomorrow

we offer

our

hands

as human

beings

remember us

WINTER SOLSTICE

For a few hours
once a year,
we are in alignment
moon earth sun
mind body soul
and can look back
into the center
of our galaxy.
For a few hours
once a year,
we are the closest
to the center
of our galaxy
and in alignment
with the
source of life
source of spirit.
In an instant,
it seems to us,
the sun stands still
and we are in
transformation
a concentration of power
as we see
into the center
and know our place
in the stars.

WETU

HENA UŊKIKSUYAPI

We are Star People. Wicaŋhpi Oyate heuŋtaŋhaŋpi.

Our legacy is as diverse, as present, as absent as

stars in the sky. In the brilliant light of day,

we see just one star, our Sun, but those

other stars are not gone. At sunset,

they appear again. Bright city

lights may darken them

but they are not gone.

Our point of

reference

veils

or

clears

our vision.

To create beauty

from tragedy, healing

from trauma is not a battle

for supremacy of a single story

but a process of new understandings

that evolve as we evolve. But where does

"true memory" reside? Our past is recorded in

our way of life, in our traditions, and in the living

hearts of our people. Our stories shine there like stars.

And we remember those.

BDOTE ON THE EDGE OF SPRING

Rush through this place,
a grey-brown world where
winter still clenches
broken branches,
bark chewed from fallen trees.
Watermarks high on trunks
mark floods from years before.
White plastic buckets under
blue taps are ready
for the sap to flow.
Cardinal splashes red among
the grey branches,
red buds bursting,
red tobacco ties waving.
Green sprouts among last year's leaves,
pale yellow wood chips glint
in the sun where beavers
cut trees near the river.
Then above the ridge,
a single bird calls
wetu wetu
and it is almost spring.

RISING

morning song rises
above frost covered earth
disperses in the sun

migratory paths
follow rivers winds
imprinted on land by time

cell memories carry
genetic experience
in heart blood bone

strength of the generations
tender as lilacs
returns in spring song

AT FLANDREAU STATE PARK

A small white stone
proclaims here
    HERE
  was the born the first
    white child
      in
    Minnesota.
Date verified. Witnesses.
No monument erected.
No obelisks.
No great rotunda or basilica.
A small white stone,
a remnant of snow at its base.
Yet all around are thousands
    upon
   thousands
   times
   thousands
of small brown stones
bearing witness that here
    HERE
  were born the first
   children
    in
  Mni Sota Makoce.

The first word
whispered
into their ears
by their mothers
danikota.
Lullabies heard first
in Dakota,
the cries of joy,
exclamations of beauty,
and welcome heard first.
Wakaŋiża
they are holy,

like God.

AT JEFFERS

We stand among
wildflowers
in crevices
of quartzite,
growing from seeds
carried by summer floods,
dropped by migrating birds,
blown by blizzard winds.
We follow the path
on softer ground
of small racoon prints,
deer tracks,
pale green moss,
a white spiral shell
pressed into mud,
so many shades
of brown.
We take root
nourished by stories
of those who
grew here
first.

AT FORT SNELLING STATE PARK

Yesterday, a mouse
struggled in a sharp black trap
in the pavilion
near the Visitor Center
as people walked to the door.

It was tired and weak
so I gently stroked its back,
there in the soft grass,
sang for it and set it free.
Mitakuye owasiŋ.

SPRING DISPLAY

Dawn lifts the night sky.
Blackbird songs fill the ravine
where the river flows.
The first daffodils emerge
as spring slips across the land.

Cold loses its grip
on the rolling open land.
A pair of geese honks,
their two young ones close behind
rising in the morning light.

1918 PANDEMIC GHOST

A stranger came up
the road to her grandma's house
near Malloy Hollow
at the back edge of the woods
on the Post Road close to Bunch.

It appeared quickly
as she and her sister played
in their grandma's yard,
pigs rooting near the split-rail
fence for a cool place to lay.

She ran to the woods
when Liza screamed, "Vgilv!
Asgili, nula!"
They were too afraid to move,
to even whisper, unsure

where their grandma was
as the figure drew closer.
With white hair and skin,
its legs covered by white boots,
a long, white cape flowed behind.

As the ghost came close,
they heard the screen door open
as their grandma stepped
out onto the porch to stand.
They were too afraid to breathe.

Then she spoke to it.

And it spoke to her.

They could not hear what was said.

> Does anyone in your house have the flu?
> Is anyone coughing? Feverish?
> Have you been to Stilwell?
> Nine people died there last week from the Spanish Flu.
> The schools are being closed. Have you been to Tahlequah?
> 14,000 people in Tahlequah have the flu.

When the voices stopped,
the girls came to the corner
of the house and looked
down the road to see the ghost
float away in the fall breeze.

Their grandma called them
up to the porch of the house.
"People are dying,
even more people are sick.
It is a very bad thing.

That nurse came to say
we must be very careful."
They were more afraid,
she and her sister Liza,
of the first ghost white person

they had ever seen.

WAŊNA WETU

Waŋna wetu u
waȟpe yuġaŋ ayapi
zitkada sapa
witaya heyapi
hehan owas dowaŋpi.

Early signs of spring
are appearing every day.
Buds swelling on trees,
grass greening across the yard,
blackbirds singing in the sun.

AŊPETU TECA HECA

Odowaŋ ota
nawaȟuŋ hehan wekta
k'a iyomakpi.
Aŋpetu teca heca.
Zitkada e dowaŋpi.

At dawn, I awoke
to the sound of bird songs
floating on the breeze,
the promise of a new day
carried in their melody.

WIYAKA SKA

Wiyaka ska e
caga ed wabdake
owaŋyagwaśte
cistiŋna kʼa waśtena
wi kiŋ ed oyakpakpa.

On my morning walk,
I see feathers in the ice
sparkling in the sun,
small and beautiful they shine
all along the gravel road.

WAȞCA ZIZI

Zitkada ota
maka akan yaŋkapi
ake wa hiŋhe
tka hnuȟ wetu heca k'a
waȟca zi icaǧapi.

Gray sky hides the sun.
Birds blink and stay near the ground
as snow flies sideways.
Daffodils keep pushing up
toward the promise of spring.

WIKCEMNA SAM WIKCEMNA

FROM ARTICLE 10 OF THE TREATY OF FORT LARAMIE, 29 APRIL 1869

From time to time,
    year to year,

taku dena owas
    uŋkiksuyapi kte

in lieu of all treaties
    heretofore made

wowapi owas
    uŋkaġapi ded

and the manner
    of their delivery,

dena sdoduŋyapi
    k'a uŋkokaħniġapi

in testimony of all
    which we receive

taku owas uŋciŋpi
    uŋyuhapi kte

each person, each family,
    each lodge

tuwe dena owas
    wicauŋkiksuyapi kte

shall be named,
    entitled to be present

waŋna

four years, 12 years,
    14 years, 30 years,

tokatakiya

in no event withdrawn or
    discontinued,

ohiŋni

each lodge, each family
    settled

taku dena owas
    ecuŋk'uŋpi kte

permanently.

heuŋ uŋnipi kte.

WIKCEMNA SAM WIKCEMNA

taku dena owas
    uŋkiksuyapi kte

wowapi owas
    uŋkaǵapi ded

dena sdoduŋyapi
    k'a uŋkokaḣniǵapi

taku owas uŋciŋpi
    uŋyuhapi kte

tuwe dena owas
    wicauŋkiksuyapi kte

waŋna

tokatakiya

ohiŋni

taku dena owas
    ecuŋk'uŋpi kte

heuŋ uŋnipi kte.

TEN BY TEN

We will remember
    these things

all the words
    written here

we know and
    understand them

We will have everything
    we need

We will remember
    these people

now

in the future

always

We do these
    things

so we will live.

BDOKETU

SUMMER SOLSTICE

Soybean fields shimmer
in the bright afternoon light
when the sun stands still.
A single tundra swan waits
among the rows staring north.

Standing immobile,
stark white in the summer field
·now more gold than green,
a heron gazes beyond
the tree line expectantly.

Waiting and watching,
perhaps listening to songs
of frogs and locusts
along the Maple River,
balanced between earth and sky.

OYAṪE WAŚAKAPI

Ded oyaṫe waśaka maniṗi tka
Ticaġaṗi kʼa caŋku kaġaṗi itokab
Maka kiŋ wouŋkʼuṗi
Su ożuṗi hena uŋkiyeṗi
Okṗaza kʼa ożaŋżaŋ etaŋhaŋ wouŋkʼuṗi

Naṗe hena maka kiŋ kicaŋyaṗi
Tohaŋ maka ṗuza, mnitaŋ, hewaŋke kʼa taku ide
Kʼaś taku owas icaġe
Wasutoŋṗi kʼa waokiyaṗi uŋsṗeṗi
Hnuḣ ded oyaṫe waśaka maniṗi

LA GENTE FUERTE

La gente fuerte caminó aquí
Mucho antes que el hormigón y el acero
Nutrido por la tierra
Somos las semillas plantaron
Alimentadas por la oscuridad y la luz

Manos esperanzadas trabajan el suelo
En sequía y inundación, helada y fuego
Creciendo juntos
Compartiendo su cosecha con amor
La gente fuerte está caminando aquí

STRONG PEOPLE

Strong people walked here
Long before concrete and steel
Nourished by the earth
We are the seeds they planted
Fed by darkness and by light
Hopeful hands work soil
In drought and flood, frost and fire
Growing together
Sharing their harvest with love
Strong people are walking here

FLINT HILLS SCENIC BYWAY

Much of the land along the byway
remains as it has been
for thousands of years,
the brochure says.
Cattle roam wide across four directions,
as far as the eye can see.

Heron floats gracefully,
hawk soars high,
faceless windmill appears
coming over the first rise,
tires sing on the asphalt.
This place breathes free.

Wide open, rolling spaces.
Cottonwoods glint,
meadowlarks sing from a fence wire.
Horses, yellow and black,
among the cottonwoods
drink at the edge of a pond.

A restored antelope herd
appears above the rise
with the morning sun.
May this ancient place remain
for thousands of years
after we are long gone.

BILLBOARD WARNING

Racing down the interstate

music blaring   tires humming

landscapes and billboards

    blur

unnoticed by uncaring carloads

intent on getting somewhere

sooner than later

    then

there on the right in

white against black

ominous words six feet high

    flash

in the twinkling of an eye

    WHEN YOU DIE

    YOU WILL SEE GOD Hebrews 9:27

knee jerk   whiplash

    deceleration

to meet the posted speed limit

not the heavenly destination

    then

there on the left in

black against white

menacing words six feet high

    glare

in a sarcastic tone

    HAVE A GOOD DAY

A PLACE FOR DREAMS

Quilts were made to be used
    on a bed, as a bed on the floor
        on the ground, in the car
two folded quilts under us
    is what grandma called a "pallet"
        laid on cool grass in hot weather
handmade, hand stitched, hand quilted
    so many stitches, so many hands
        so many dreams
Sleep is restorative
    let go
        breathe deeply
            without sleep
                there are no dreams
                    without dreams there are no answers
Sheets dried on a clothesline
    smell like sunshine
        and can clear the clutter
of a tired mind weighed down
    by never-ending
        meaningless details
Dreams and sleep
    are the dreamers
        in their beds?
if we have no bed
    can we still
        dream?
            We must hold on to our beds
                hold on to our quilts
                    and hold on to our dreams

CELESTIAL PERSPECTIVE

The Perseids streak
across the deep Milky Way,
blaze orange and white,
serenaded by crickets,
then disappear in dawn's light.
Cosmic loneliness,
the need to find life out there,
to not be alone,
our planet just one among
more than we can imagine.
Formed from cosmic dust,
trillions of universes
in our galaxy,
our singularity is
the opposite of a star.
Our minute planet
remains the one place we know
that can sustain us,
the limit of our knowledge
expanding not receding.

SHIFTING CADENCE

Birds no longer sing at dawn.
The cricket chorus
chants to greet the rising sun
as locusts join in
harmony to greet the day.

Yellow waves wash across fields
of deep green soybeans.
The sun now rises due east
over the tree line.
Dew hangs heavy in the grass.

LATE SUMMER RESPITE

Rain dripping from the tree tops.
Blackbirds and wrens sing.
Thunder rolls in the distance.
Parched earth relaxes
and breathes a sigh of relief.

Full moon glows golden orange,
a perfect circle.
Saturn and Jupiter shine
in opposition
as the sky deepens to black.

WOCEKIYA WAŊ

After heavy storms and wind,
a headless rabbit
lays on the side of the road.
How do we go on
when there is no reason why?

Crows circle above the trees
squawking an alarm,
an intruder in their midst
there in the ravine.
Dark clouds obscure the sunrise.

I move the rabbit's body
and place it among
tall grass flattened by the rain
and fallen branches,
and make prayers for us all.

ODOWAŊ TOKAHEYA

Retracing the steps
of my Dakota ancestors
along a route
to commemorate
their forced march,
I sang these words
before I knew what they
meant,

before I knew the history
of the women,
the children,
the old people,
the families
in the aftermath
of the war—
that war.

Maka siŋtomni
Dakod wicohaŋ kiŋ oteḣike
Ina Ate damakota keyepca
Mnihed mic'iye

Marking each mile
with a prayer stick,
speaking the names

of the families,
singing this song
one hundred and fifty times
in seven days,
for six years.

My grandma
died before
I was born,
yet her grandma's
grandma's stories,
imprinted in
my cell memory, were

re-membered.

BREATHE DEEP AND SING

We sing for the mussels,
we, the otters and beavers, the frogs and dragonflies,
the waterbirds and songbirds, the coyotes too.
We breathe deep, and sing for the mussels
who are the lungs of the Mississippi River.
Our river—polluted by
sewage and wastewater,
dredged and dammed,
pockmarked by dead zones
of chemicals and dyes,
banked by the edge
of destruction.
Our river—
a global super-flyway,
it flows through the heart of us,
flowed through the heart of us
for centuries, beyond centuries,
beyond memory.
Through wetlands and backwaters,
communities and economies,
plagued by invasive species,
invasive humans—
environmental degradation
that flowed through the heart of us.
Our river—
It calls to us, it beckons us,
our dreams flow along with it.

So, we sing for the mussels,

we, the otters and beavers, the frogs and dragonflies,

the waterbirds and songbirds, the coyotes too.

We breathe deep and sing for the mussels

who are the silent sentinels of our river.

They hold the stories and the pain of

our river—40, 70, 200 years ago.

Like the trees above them

along the banks of

our river, the rings of the mussels' shells

are a living record of our environment

and of our river.

They mark the resilience,

the struggles, the restoration

of floodplains and river bottoms,

the restoration of health and hearts.

How do we heal our river

without healing ourselves?

Our river—

It calls to us, it beckons us,

our dreams flow along with it.

Its water shapes us, embraces us,

and is our first medicine.

So, we sing for the mussels,

we, the otters and beavers, the frogs and dragonflies,

the waterbirds and songbirds, the coyotes too.

Breathe deep and sing with us for the mussels.

And we will sing for you.

DAKOTA LANGUAGE

Dakota people have been reading and writing in their own language since at least the 1830s, when they collaborated with the Protestant missionaries to translate the Bible into Dakota. They were multilingual, speaking French, Latin, English, Odawa, Anishinaabemowin, HoChunk, and other Indigenous languages. Before that, they were recording ideas in written form using symbols or pictographs on birchbark and other smooth surfaces.

CHEROKEE LANGUAGE

Cherokee people have also been writing in their own language since the early 19th century. By 1821, Sequoyah—in Cherokee, ᏍᏆᏯ —had developed a writing system that was later adapted to the printing press. The *Cherokee Phoenix* newspaper, printed in Cherokee and English and launched in 1828, was the first Native American newspaper in the United States.

NOTES

"Covalent Bonds": A covalent bond is created when two atoms share an electron. It is the strongest chemical bond.

"First Song": The Cherokee language used in this poem is the first verse of the hymn "Amazing Grace," taught to me by my grandma Nellie Mae Bunch Johnson.

"Oyaṫe Waṡakaṗi," "La Gente Fuerte," and "Strong People" are included in the Field Museum's new permanent exhibit *Native Truths: Our Voices, Our Stories*. Fun fact: these poems can be read from top to bottom and from bottom to top.

"Odowaŋ Tokaheya" includes the Dakota song taught to me by my tuŋwiŋ Phyllis Redday Roberts.

ACKNOWLEDGMENTS

Many thanks to the team at Holy Cow! Press for bringing this collection from draft and dream to reality.

Thanks also to the editors of the following publications where my poems have previously appeared in print: "Crow Knows" and "Giving Thanks" in *Yellow Medicine Review* (Spring 2014); and "Wikcemna Sam Wikcemna" in *Articles of a Treaty: 1868 Fort Laramie Treaty Poetry Chapbook* (2019); "Covalent Bonds" in *Rocked by the Waters: Poems of Motherhood* (2020); "Breathe Deep and Sing" in *Red Wing Arts 21st Annual Poet Artist Collaboration* (2022).

ᎬᏙ to Roy Boney, Jr. (ᎣᎲᏍ ᎠᏇᏉ) for "The Musician." It is an honor to have his work grace the cover of this collection.

My sister poet/artist Adriana Gordillo reviewed my Spanish translations and inspires me with our spirited conversations about words and art and the world in general.

Wambdi Wapaha, taku owas wakaġe hena waśte eciŋeś hena Wakaŋ Taŋka etaŋhaŋ k'a eciŋeś ohiŋni misakib nayaẑiŋ ce'e.

My children Travis and Erin, you heard some of these stories from your grandma and great-grandma for longer than you can remember. Keep them close in your hearts.

And Violet and Scarlet, this book is also for you. May you always know where your songs come from.

ABOUT THE AUTHOR

Gwen Nell Westerman is a poet, a visual artist, and a scholar. Her roots are deep in the landscape of the tallgrass prairie and reveal themselves in her art and writing. Her father's family is from Heipa District of the Sisseton Wahpeton Oyate, and her mother's family is from the Flint District of the Cherokee Nation. Neither of her parents spoke English when they were sent as small children to boarding schools in Oklahoma and South Dakota, and they met at Haskell Indian Institute in 1953. Gwen understands from experience the important way language shapes who we are. She was appointed as the Poet Laureate of Minnesota in 2021.

Her poetry is included in *Native Truths: Our Voices, Our Stories* at the Field Museum in Chicago, and has appeared recently in *Yellow Medicine Review* (Fall 2022); *When the Light of the World Was Subdued, Our Songs Came Through: A Norton Anthology of Native Nations Poetry* (2020); *POETRY* Magazine (2019); and *New Poets of Native Nations: 21 Poets of the 21st Century* (2018).

Her award-winning visual art is included in *Quiltfolk Issue 13—Minnesota* (2019) and *Sewing & Survival: Native American Quilts from 1880-2022* by Teresa Duryea Wong. Her quilts are in the permanent collections of the Minnesota Historical Society, the Great Plains Art Museum, The Heritage Center of the Red Cloud Indian School, and The University Art Galleries at the University of South Dakota. For more information, please visit *www.gwenwesterman.com*